D1505013

OCEANS

UNDERWATER WORLDS

by Laura Purdie Salas   illustrated by Jeff Yesh

Thanks to our advisers for their expertise, research, and advice:

Michael T. Lares, Ph.D., Associate Professor of Biology
University of Mary, Bismarck, North Dakota

Susan Kesselring, M.A., Literacy Educator
Rosemount–Apple Valley–Eagan (Minnesota) School District

PICTURE WINDOW BOOKS
Minneapolis, Minnesota

Editor: Jill Kalz

Designers: Joe Anderson and Hilary Wacholz

Page Production: Melissa Kes

Art Director: Nathan Gassman

Associate Managing Editor: Christianne Jones

The illustrations in this book were created digitally.

Picture Window Books

151 Good Counsel Drive, P.O. Box 669

Mankato, Minnesota 56002.

www.capstonepub.com

Printed in the United States of America in North America, Minnesota.

072010   005866R

 Books published by Capstone Press are manufactured with paper
containing at least 10 percent post-consumer waste.

Library of Congress Cataloging-in-Publication Data

Salas, Laura Purdie.

Oceans : underwater worlds / by Laura Purdie Salas ; illustrated by Jeff Yesh.

p. cm.

Includes bibliographical references and index.

ISBN-13: 978-1-4048-3097-4 (library binding)

ISBN-10: 1-4048-3097-9 (library binding)

ISBN-13: 978-1-4048-3471-2 (paperback)

ISBN-10: 1-4048-3471-0 (paperback)

1. Marine biology—Juvenile literature. 2. Ocean—Juvenile literature.

I. Yesh, Jeff, 1971– ill. II. Title.

QH91.16.S25 2007

578.77—dc22   2006027215

Table of Contents

The World Ocean

What words do you think of when you hear the word *ocean*? How about *big*, *salty*, and *wet*? The ocean is a big, salty, wet ecosystem. An ecosystem is all of the living and nonliving things in a certain area. It includes plants, animals, water, soil, weather … everything!

Five oceans make up the ocean ecosystem. The largest is the Pacific Ocean. It is as big as all of Earth's land put together! The other oceans are the Atlantic, the Indian, the Arctic, and the Southern. All of the oceans are connected.

FUN FACT

The ocean floor is made up of many different landforms. There are mountains, plains, slopes, volcanoes, and long, narrow ditches called trenches. The deepest point in the ocean lies within the Mariana Trench in the western Pacific. There, it is nearly 7 miles (11 kilometers) from the water's surface to the ocean floor.

The ocean has thousands of different kinds of fish. They can be found just below the ocean's surface, on the ocean floor, and everywhere in between.

Fish have fins and gills. Fins help fish swim, and gills help them breathe. Fish need oxygen, just like people do, but they breathe underwater. Water holds oxygen. As water flows over a fish's gills, oxygen is pulled in for the fish to use.

FUN FACT

Sharks are a kind of fish. Unlike other fish, however,
sharks do not have a bony skeleton. Their skeleton is
made of cartilage. Cartilage is the bendable material
that human noses are made of.

Invertebrates and Mammals

Most of the animals in the ocean are invertebrates. Invertebrates do not have a backbone. They range from hard-shelled lobsters and clams to spiny sea stars, from octopuses and jellyfish to sponges and colorful corals.

Mammals also live in the ocean. Mammals make their own body heat and bear live young. They must breathe air. Dolphins and whales are ocean mammals. They come to the surface to breathe through the blowhole on top of their heads. Other ocean mammals include sea lions, walruses, and sea otters.

FUN FACT

Lots of other animals live in the ocean, too. Reptiles such as sea turtles, sea snakes, and crocodiles live there. Many seabirds, such as penguins, gulls, and pelicans, spend some time in the water and some time out of the water.

9

Tiny Plants, Tall Plants

The most common ocean plants are so little that you cannot see them. Plankton are some of Earth's smallest living things. Many large animals, such as whales, feed on these tiny, drifting plants.

Kelp is the ocean's largest plant. It can reach 300 feet (91 meters) from the ocean floor. Fish like to hide in forests of kelp. Because of that, seals and sea lions often hunt nearby.

FUN FACT

Seagrass forms meadows in shallow waters.
It has roots that get food from the ocean floor.
Many fish lay their eggs in seagrass.

11

The Ocean in Motion

Many things cause the ocean to move. Wind blows water into waves. The waves travel until they hit land, or shore. Then the tops of the waves curl over and break.

The moon and sun cause ocean tides. Their gravity pulls on the ocean as Earth spins. During high tide, ocean water reaches far up onshore. During low tide, the water does not reach as far.

High Tide

Low Tide

FUN FACT

Tsunamis are giant, powerful waves caused by earthquakes.
They are not caused by winds, tides, or currents.

13

North
America

Atlantic
Ocean

South
America

Flowing Currents

Ocean water also moves in currents.
Currents can flow from one large area of land
toward another. They can also flow from the
surface of the ocean to deeper water. The wind
causes surface currents. Currents below the
surface are caused by changes in water
temperature and saltiness.

Southern
Ocean

Arctic
Ocean

Asia

Europe

Warm Currents
Cold Currents

Pacific
Ocean

Africa

EQUATOR

Indian
Ocean

Australia

FUN FACT

The Gulf Stream is a warm ocean current. It starts in the
Gulf of Mexico and travels around Florida. Then it moves
north along the coast of the United States. The Gulf
Stream flows at about 4 miles (6 kilometers) per hour.

Antarctica

Salty Seas

The oceans have always been salty. Long ago, heavy rains fell on the dry Earth for millions of years. The water formed rivers. The rivers picked up salt as they ran over rocks and soil. The rivers flowed to low areas and made the oceans salty.

FUN FACT

The more salt water has in it, the more easily you can float. That means
it's easier for you to float in the ocean than in a swimming pool.

17

Water Cycle

The ocean supplies the world with water. People, plants, and animals need water to survive. All life on Earth depends on the ocean's water cycle.

When the sun heats the ocean, water on the ocean's surface changes into a gas. The gas floats up into the air and forms droplets. Those droplets later fall to the ground as rain or snow. Rivers carry the water back to the ocean, and the water cycle begins again.

FUN FACT

During the ocean's water cycle, only the water changes into a gas and floats into the air. The salt stays in the ocean. That's why rain isn't salty.

Ocean in Danger

Everyone needs the ocean ecosystem, but sometimes people do things that harm it. They fish too much, until some kinds of fish disappear forever. They build along the water's edge and destroy animal homes. They pollute the water.

Today, many people are working hard to protect the ocean. But much work still needs to be done. It's important to care for all of Earth's ecosystems. Together, they make our beautiful blue planet an amazing place to live!

FUN FACT

The ocean has many gifts. It provides fish and other seafood for people around the world. Some of its plants and animals are used to make medicines. Oil beneath the ocean floor can be turned into gasoline.

21

Ocean Diorama: Ocean in a Box

WHAT YOU NEED:

- a shoebox
- colored paper
- scissors
- tape
- glue
- sand
- thread
- pictures of fish and other ocean animals

WHAT YOU DO:

1. First, turn the shoebox on its side.

2. Line the inside of the box with blue paper.

3. Spread a very thin layer of glue over the bottom. Then sprinkle sand over the glue and let it dry. Shake off the extra sand.

4. Now, create your ocean scene. Include some fish, mammals, and ocean reptiles. Use colored paper or pictures to make them. Use the thread to hang a few of the animals from the top of the box. It will look like they're swimming!

Ocean Facts

- Water covers almost three-fourths of Earth's surface. Most of that water—97 percent—is in the oceans.

- The average depth of the ocean is 12,200 feet (3,700 m)—or a little over 2 miles (3.2 km).

- Sunlight cannot reach deeper than 3,300 feet (1,001 m) in the ocean. Below that level lies the midnight zone. It is completely black there. Some fish in the midnight zone, such as hatchet fish and viper fish, light up like fireflies. The light helps them see their food.

- The blue whale is the largest animal ever to live on Earth. It is even bigger than any known dinosaur. The blue whale can grow to more than 100 feet (30 m) long and weigh up to 150 tons (135 metric tons). One blue whale can weigh as much as two houses!

Glossary

current—when a stream of ocean water flows in a certain direction

ecosystem—an area with certain animals, plants, weather, and land or water features

gravity—the force that pulls objects toward Earth's surface

invertebrates—animals that do not have backbones

mammals—warm-blooded animals that feed their young milk

oxygen—a gas that all humans, animals, and plants need to live

reptiles—cold-blooded animals with a backbone and scales

water cycle—the process of ocean water becoming rain around the world

To Learn More

AT THE LIBRARY

Ganeri, Anita. *I Wonder Why the Sea Is Salty: And Other Questions About the Oceans.* Boston: Kingfisher, 2003.

Gray, Samantha. *Ocean.* New York: Dorling Kindersley, 2001.

Jackson, Kay. *Oceans.* Mankato, Minn.: Bridgestone Books, 2006.

ON THE WEB

FactHound offers a safe, fun way to find Web sites related to this book. All of the sites on FactHound have been researched by our staff.

1. Visit *www.facthound.com*
2. Type in this special code: 1404830979
3. Click on the FETCH IT button.

Your trusty FactHound will fetch the best sites for you!

Index

LOOK FOR ALL OF THE BOOKS IN THE AMAZING SCIENCE— ECOSYSTEMS SERIES:

Deserts: Thirsty Wonderlands

Grasslands: Fields of Green and Gold

Oceans: Underwater Worlds

Rain Forests: Gardens of Green

Temperate Deciduous Forests: Lands of Falling Leaves

Wetlands: Soggy Habitat